M . C . ESCHER

T&J

This edition published 2009

Published by
TAJ BOOKS INTERNATIONAL LLP
27 Ferndown Gardens
Cobham
Surrey
KT11 2BH
UK
www.tajbooks.com

All notations of errors or omissions (author inquiries, permissions) concerning the content of this book should be addressed to info@tajbooks.com.

All enquiries regarding the works of M.C. Escher should be directed to:

Cordon Art B.V.
P.O.Box 101
3740 AC Baarn
the Netherlands
Tel: + 31-(0)35-541.80.41
Fax: +31-(035)-541.17.66
Website: www.mcescher.com
Email: info@mcescher.com

ISBN: 978-1-84406-123-5

M . C . ESCHER

BY SANDRA FORTY

CONTENTS

MAURITS CORNELIS ESCHER 1898-1972

To enter the world of M.C. Escher is to set foot into unknown and unsettling territory. His extraordinary pictures of logic and perspective fool the brain into believing the impossible—that staircases can climb forever, that fish can morph into birds, and that water can run uphill. His unique vision created extraordinary images that are instantly recognisable as being from his hand.

Escher, who was left-handed, drew and sketched compulsively from a young age and left over 2,000 drawings and 448 lithographs, woodcuts, and engravings. He became skilled in many printing techniques including woodcuts, lithographs, and mezzotints. He achieved great success in his lifetime and as well as his numerous prints he was asked to illustrate books, posters, murals, ceramic tiles, tapestries, and postage stamps. His legacy is carefully guarded by the M.C. Escher Foundation at Baarn, The Netherlands.

A great deal is known about him because Escher was a regular and prolific letter writer, especially to members of his family, as well as to friends and customers. As Escher was in the habit of making copies of his letters they remain an invaluable source of information about him, his moods, and his thought processes throughout his life.

Another life-long habit was that of taking regular sea voyages—often on freighters—and usually around the Mediterranean. He would disembark at port and while the ship unloaded and loaded cargo, he would visit the nearby towns and countryside before re-embarking for the next leg of the voyage. These adventures inspired and relaxed him in a way nothing else could. All the while he would make numerous sketches that he used as a basis for his work later in the year.

Throughout his life Escher was often frustrated and even depressed at his own perceived inability to work out a particular puzzle or difficult visual idea. But he would work at it and lose sleep over the problem until he finally hit on how to produce the picture. To help himself he would make 3-D models of constructs that he wished to draw so that he could work out the angles, vanishing points and other details.

His method of working, principally woodcuts, was very time consuming, as was the final printing process. Many of his prints required up to five blocks, each used a number of times with varying intensity of inks. As he got more skilled with woodcutting, he was able to work more quickly and he could design and complete each piece in a much shorter time. However, as he became more successful at selling his work, he found he was forced to put aside his innovative work to print up more copies of pieces he had done. This constriction of his time he found frustrating and he would periodically instruct his agents to put up the prices of his prints to stem the flow of orders. The ploy rarely worked.

Escher was a stunning graphic illustrator, especially of landscape and architecture—and in particular of Italian hilltop towns. In fact Italy was a great inspiration to Escher and a country to which he repeatedly returned. These early "straight" works are often overlooked even though many of them show his early fascination with unusual space and perspectives.

Maurits Cornelis Escher, known affectionately as Mauk, was born on June 17, 1898 in the Dutch town of Leeuwarden in the province of Friesland. He was the youngest of five sons of George, a civil engineer, and his much younger (by 17 years) second wife, Sarah. Significantly, it was while at secondary school in Arnhem that the young Maurits was taught how to make linocuts by his art teacher, F.W. van der Haagen.

As a boy he was creative and his imagination ever active—he reportedly saw such things as identifiable shapes in the clouds. But, apart from art Escher did not distinguish himself at school and he failed all his exams except for mathematics. Out of school time he was already experimenting with printing techniques with his lifelong friend Bas Kist who he met at catechism class aged 15.

He next attended the Higher Technical School in Delft (1918–19) but he was already spending much of his time making small woodcuts rather than studying. He suffered from poor health, was painfully thin, and was easily tired by exercise. At last allowed to leave his school education, he enrolled at the School for Architecture and Decorative Arts in Haarlem. There his artistic talent was quickly noted, and following the recommendation of his graphics teacher, Samuel Jessurum de Mesquita, he sought permission from the Director and his parents to devote himself entirely to the decorative arts, principally woodcuts.

Escher visited Italy, first with his family and then with friends. After returning home he was soon traveling again, this time to Alicante in Spain. He visited Madrid and the Prado, but his greatest inspiration came from Granada and the grand 14th century Alhambra palace, where he was particularly taken with the complex Islamic decorations. He had become interested in the regular division of the plane and now seeing the Islamic patterns revived his interest and set him thinking about regular division again. But he found this work both slow and frustrating and gave it up for some years.

Escher soon left Holland for an extended visit to Italy. While there he traveled extensively, sketched, and worked hard at his woodcuts. He wrote home to his friends and family of his happy times. He started keeping a visual diary of sketches with the idea of improving his technique through regular practice. While in Italy he met and fell in love with Jetta Umiker, the daughter of a German-Swiss industrialist. Escher's first one-man show was held in Siena between August 13–16, 1923, but at the time he was far more concerned with his pursuit of Jetta than his exhibition. By now he had grown his trademark beard—a subject of much humorous comment within his family.

In November Jetta and her family moved to Rome and Escher went too. They planned a spring wedding but were warned by a doctor not to have children until Jetta had put on weight and gained strength. Escher's first exhibition in his homeland was held to quite good reviews in February 1924 at the De Zonnebloem art gallery in The Hague.

At last Mauk and Jetta were married in Viareggio on June 12, 1924, in the town hall. They honeymooned in Switzerland before traveling around Europe, buying an apartment in Rome. Throughout winter 1926 and spring 1927 Escher worked hard preparing for an exhibition in the galleries of the Association of Roman Engravers, at the Palazzetto Venezia, Rome. He exhibited some 40 or so drawings, a series of six woodcuts of the Days of the Creation, plus 16 additional woodcuts. The reviews were favorable and the exhibition was well reported back home in Holland.

On July 23, 1926, the Escher's first son, George, was born. They needed a larger house and found one nearby. It provided a studio for Escher, on the fourth floor. His fame as a graphic artist was growing in the second half of the 1920s and his work featured in a number of exhibitions: Arnhem and Amsterdam in 1926; Amsterdam, 1927; Leiden 1928; Rotterdam, Utrecht, Leeuwarden, Arnhem, and The Hague, 1929.

Generally well received and admired for its structural qualities and technique, some critics were concerned about his lack of spontaneity. But by now his prints were being sought by dealers and he was managing to make a reasonable living from his woodcuts.

Escher returned to Italy at every opportunity. In the 1920s he undertook spring trips around the remoter regions by train, mule, and walking. Their purpose was for pleasure but also to gather sketches and reference material and inspiration for his work later in the year.

On December 8, 1928, his second son, Arthur, was born. At around this time Escher decided to try his hand at lithography again. He asked his former art teacher, Mr. Dieperink, to help him. But in spite of his best efforts he still could not make a comfortable living. His confidence in his work was diminishing because he could not sell his pictures. His health was too fragile for extended work and was slowly getting worse. Furthermore, his family also suffered from poor health.

Fortunately, help was at hand from the noted art historian G.J. Hoogewerff, Director of the Dutch Historical Institute in Rome, who encouraged Escher and wrote an article about his graphics in the October 1931 issue of Elsevier's Geïllustreerd Maandschrift. He applauded Escher's work as cerebral but also humorous.

In midsummer 1931 the Escher family journeyed to The Hague. While there Escher discovered the artistic virtues of using end-grain wood for making engravings for his prints from the wood engraver Fokko Mees. He immediately set about developing the new technique. At last his work was selling, albeit moderately and mostly at home in Holland. A few commissions were landing at his door, and his work was starting to sell in the United States: at the Exhibition of Contemporary Prints held at the Art Institute of Chicago his print "Nonza" won third prize.

In summer 1935 the family decided to move to Switzerland—in part due to the increasingly difficult political situation in Italy, where the Fascists were coming to the forefront of Italian politics. They left in July 1935 to rent an isolated farmhouse in Château-d'Oex. Escher still traveled a great deal, but was working hard all the while.

In April 1936 Escher made a series of voyages along the Mediterranean coast by ship. He had done a deal with the Italian shipping company, Adria, that in exchange for a number of prints of the journey, which they could use as they wished, he could sail from one port to another stopping as he wanted and changing ship at will. This gave him the opportunity to visit the Alhambra again; Escher said it was "the richest source of inspiration I have ever tapped." The Islamic patterning set Escher off on his obsession with the concept of the regular division of the plane. He worked from a geometric grid and designed his own shapes to fit into the plane. He experimented with many motifs—birds, animals, insects, reptiles, and humans. He wrote, "It remains an extremely absorbing activity, a real mania to which I have become addicted, and from which I sometimes find it hard to tear myself away."

This long journey proved a turning point in Escher's life and work. It was hugely enjoyable but, more importantly, after completing his Mediterranean prints he left behind his conventional work and turned to new avenues of exploration. He returned to the problems associated with the regular division of the plane and geometrical problems and tricks with perspective—ideas and aspirations he had felt earlier but been unable to express satisfactorily. He was also obsessed with wanting to represent music in graphic terms, so much so that he was losing sleep over the problem. He would write in 1959, "By keenly confronting the enigmas that surround us, and by considering and analyzing the observations that I had made, I ended up in the domain of mathematics . . . I often seem to have more in common with mathematicians than with my fellow-artists."

In 1937 Escher was working on a woodcut called "Metamorphosis," about which he remarked, "The study of the regular division of the plane on a flat surface led automatically to compositions that expressed a development, a cycle, or a metamorphosis."

Escher's first real encounter with mathematics came when he showed his brother Beer—a professor of geology at Leiden University—some of his latest work. Beer immediately saw the connection between Escher's work and crystallography and recommended a number of articles which he felt would help him. Greatly interested, Escher started reading. He did not understand the mathematics but in one article he recognized the 17 plane symmetry groups described. He then taught himself the principles by which each of these groups operated and used them in his work.

This new approach fascinated him and between 1937 and 1941 he produced 43 colored drawings of periodic tilings showing a wide variety of forms. His approach was very mathematical and systematic and for this he devised his own notation system.

The Eschers moved house in late summer 1937 to a suburb of Brussels. By now expecting their third child (Jan, born the following March) and Escher was trying to work out how to get movement into his drawings and woodcuts.

In 1937 he embarked on his most ambitious project yet—a 13-foot long woodcut entitled "Metamorphosis II." This remarkable project extended his work to show a narrative of developing images morphing from one idea into the next. It starts with the word "Metamorphose" and moves through fields of squares merging into creatures, then lizards, hexagons, bees, birds, fish, birds, boats, back to fish, horses, triangles, birds, cubes, a town (Atrani in Italy), a chessboard, squares, and back to "Metamorphose" again, suggesting a never-ending circle of life.

By now Europe was at war and in late February 1941 the Escher family moved to the small village of Baarn. Escher kept working and was relatively undisturbed through the-war, during which time he drew 62 (out of a total of 137) of his Regular Division drawings.

Escher was fascinated with the regular division of the plane and its associated problems. He compiled extensive notebooks as his work progressed, filling them with his thoughts and calculations. These are produced as evidence that Escher had become a significant research mathematician. He even developed his own categorisation system that covered all the possible combinations of shape, color, and symmetrical properties. As such he unknowingly studied areas of crystallography years ahead of any professional mathematician. In commentary he wrote, "A long time ago, I chanced upon this domain [of regular division of the plane] in one of my wanderings . . . however, on the other side I landed in a wilderness . . . I came to the open gate of mathematics. Sometimes I think I have covered the whole area . . . and then I suddenly discover a new path and experience fresh delights."

Escher broke into the international consciousness with the publication of interviews with him in Time magazine of April 2, 1951, and Life of May 7, 1951. Orders for his prints started to flood in. His work was also attracting the attention of mathematicians and philosophers, intrigued with his manipulation of space and perspective. Many of these eminent people wrote to Escher and he engaged in lengthy correspondence.

At home things were difficult: Jetta was suffering from bouts of depression, so severe that their youngest son, Jan, was sent away to a children's home. It was often difficult working in these conditions that would continue until Jetta left him in 1968. However, Escher continued exhibiting and often made thoroughly prepared accompanying lectures. People flocked to hear him speak about his work and explain his unusual viewpoint: once he said, "I have often felt closer to people who work scientifically–though I certainly do not do so myself–than to my fellow-artists." Mathematicians were certainly intrigued and delighted with Escher's work. As proof of their interest a large one-man exhibition of Escher's work was held in Amsterdam's Stedelijk Museum in 1954 at the initiative of the International Mathematical Conference.

By now his work was important enough for the Whyte Gallery, Washington, to hold a one-man exhibition during late 1954. It was a great success: about a third of the prints were sold before the opening on October 7. In fact, too many orders came in and to stem the flow–because it stopped him concentrating on new projects–he drastically increased his prices. As before, it made no difference.

By 1958 Escher was trying to produce a circular division of the plane. He wrote, "A circular division of the plane, logically bordered on all sides by the infinitesimal, is something truly beautiful . . . I get the feeling that I am moving farther and farther away from work that would be a 'success' with the 'public,' but what can I do when this sort of problem fascinates me so much that I cannot leave it alone?" Involved to the point of obsession with his work Escher felt increasingly isolated from his peers. Other artists couldn't follow him into his fantasy worlds but the mathematicians, while friendly, spoke a different language.

In early 1960 Escher became interested in the concept of an endless staircase—an idea that would lead to some of his most memorable work. The following year Caroline MacGillavry, professor of crystallography at the University of Amsterdam, was so impressed with his work on the division of the plane that she wanted to have his prints published alongside her words. Their book, Symmetry Aspects of M.C. Escher's Periodic Drawings was published in 1965 under the auspices of the International Union of Crystallography. Escher was thrilled as it gave his work the seal of scientific approval and validity.

In April 1962 Escher fell ill and was admitted to hospital for an emergency operation on his stomach, forcing a trip to North America to be cancelled. In October he felt well enough to go but he fell ill almost as soon as he arrived in Canada and was rushed to hospital for another operation. He would be in and out of hospitals for the rest of his life.

In July 1969 he was working on his last woodcut "Snakes" (it took six months to complete) but by spring 1970 he was in hospital again. Too weak to do any further work he still carried on a formidable correspondence with his family and friends. He fell ill again in mid-March 1972 and was taken to hospital in Hilversum. His three sons rushed to be with him. He died on March 27, aged 73.

Plate 1

G.A. ESCHER (ESCHERS FATHER)
1916 linoleum cut
21.0 x 15.7 cm

THE BORGER OAK
1919 Linoleum cut
9.8 x 8.3cm

Plate 2

Plate 3

TREE
1919 woodcut
39.2 x 31.3cm

PLANE FILLING MOTIF WITH HUMAN FIGURES

Plate 4

1920 lithograph

43.2 x 31.2cm

Plate 5

PORTRAIT OF A MAN
1920 woodcut
34.5 x 35.0cm

JETTA (ESCHERS WIFE)

1925 woodcut
49.2 x 27.8cm

Plate 6

Plate 7

THE FALL OF MAN
1927 woodcut
37.5 x 27.6cm

Plate 8

ROME
1927 woodcut in grey and black, printed from 2 blocks
44.5 x 43.8cm

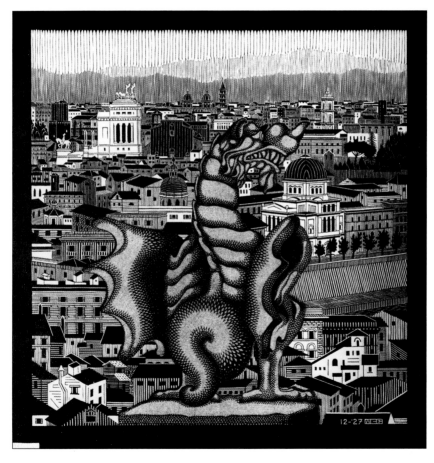

Plate 9

FARA SAN MARTINO
1928 woodcut
44.6 x 58.2cm

Plate 10

TOWER OF BABEL
1928 woodcut
62.1 x 38.6cm

Plate 11

BARBARANO, CIMINO
1929 Lithograph
17.6 x 23.6 cm

STREET IN SCANNO, ABRUZZI

1930 woodcut
62.7 x 43.1 cm

Plate 12

Plate 13

CASTROVALVA
1930 Lithograph
53.0 x 42.1 cm

Plate 14

THE BRIDGE
1930 Lithograph
53.6 x 37.7 cm

Plate 15

RAVELLO AND THE COAST OF AMALFI
1931 woodcut
31.3 x 23.7cm

Plate 16

ATRANI, COAST OF AMALFI
1931 Lithograph
27.5 x 37.9 cm

Plate 17

FARMHOUSE, RAVELLO
1932 Lithograph
23.3 x 31.1 cm

SAN MICHELE DEI FRISONI, ROME

1932 Lithograph
43.5 x 49.1 cm

Plate 18

Plate 19

LAVA FLOW OF 1928 FROM MOUNT ETNA
1933 lithograph
21.2 x 31.3cm

PHOSPHORESCENT SEA

1933 Lithograph
32.7 x 24.5cm

Plate 20

Plate 21

STILL LIFE WITH MIRROR
1934 Lithograph
39.4 x 28.7cm

STILL LIFE WITH SPHERICAL MIRROR

Plate 22

1934 Lithograph
28.6 x 32.6cm

Plate 23

HAND WITH REFLECTING SPHERE
1935 Lithograph
31.8 x 21.3cm

Plate 24

HELL, COPY AFTER HIERONYMUS BOSCH
1935 Lithograph
25.1 x 21.4 cm

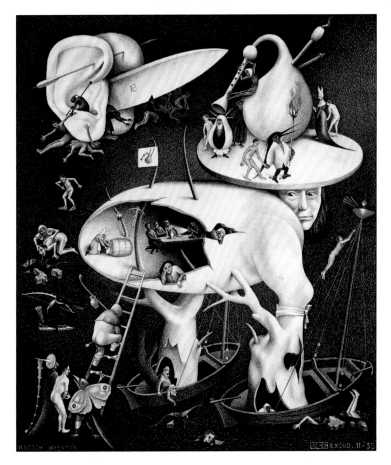

Plate 25

STILL LIFE AND STREET
1937 woodcut
48.7 x 49.0cm

Plate 26

DEVELOPMENT 1
1937 woodcut
43.7 x 44.6cm

Plate 27

METAMORPHOSIS I
1937 printed on two sheets

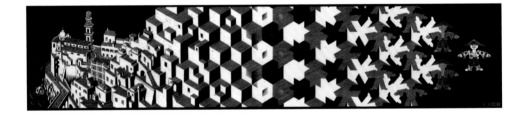

Plate 28 (right)

METAMORPHOSIS II
1940 woodcut on three sheets

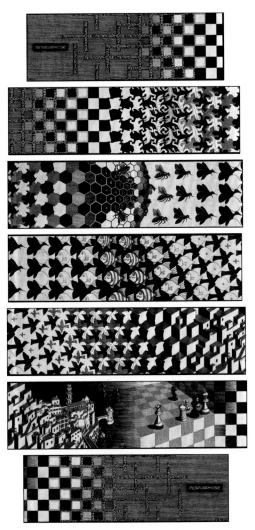

39

Plate 29

DAY AND NIGHT
1938 woodcut
39.1 x 67.7cm

Plate 30

SKY AND WATER I
1938 woodcut
43.5 x 43.9 cm

Plate 31

REPTILES
1943 Lithograph
33.4 x 38.5cm

Plate 32

THREE SPHERES I
1945 wood engraving
27.9 x 16.9 cm

Plate 33

BALCONY
1945 Lithograph
29.7 x 23.4cm

Plate 34

MAGIC MIRROR
1946 Lithograph
28.0 x 44.5 cm

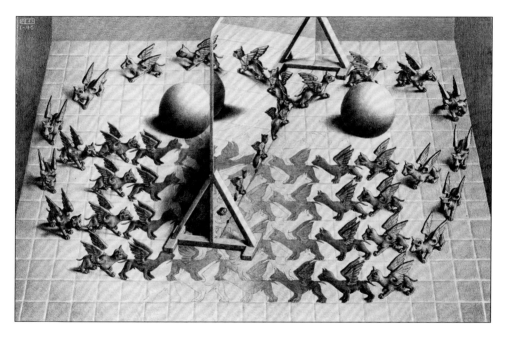

Plate 35

THREE SPHERES II
1946 Lithograph
26.9 x 46.3 cm

Plate 36

GALLERY
1946 (1st state) till 1949 (further states), Mezzotint, 4th state
21.3 x 15.9cm

Plate 37

OTHER WORLD

1947 wood engraving and woodcut in black, reddish brown, printed from 3 blocks
31.8 x 26.1cm

Plate 38

UP AND DOWN
1947 Lithograph in brown
50.3 x 20.5cm

Plate 39

HOUSE OF STAIRS
1951 Lithograph
47.2 x 23.8cm

Plate 40

DRAWING HANDS
1948 Lithograph
28.2 x 33.2cm

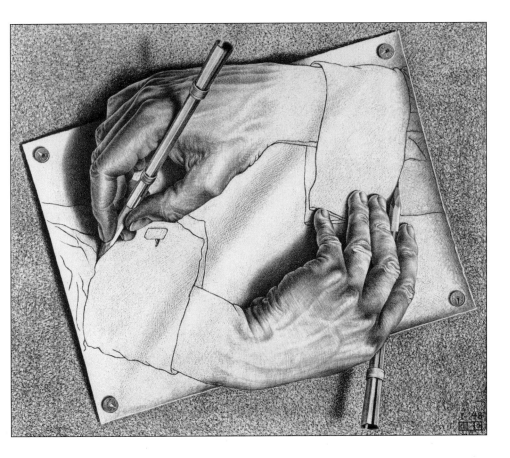

Plate 41

SUN AND MOON

1948 woodcut in blue, red, yellow and black, printed from 4 blocks
25.1 x 27.0cm

Plate 42

STARS
1948 wood engraving
32.0 x 26.0cm

Plate 43

NEW YEAR'S GREETING CARD
1949
15.2 x 13.9 cm

DOUBLE PLANETOID

1949 wood engraving
Diameter 37.4cm

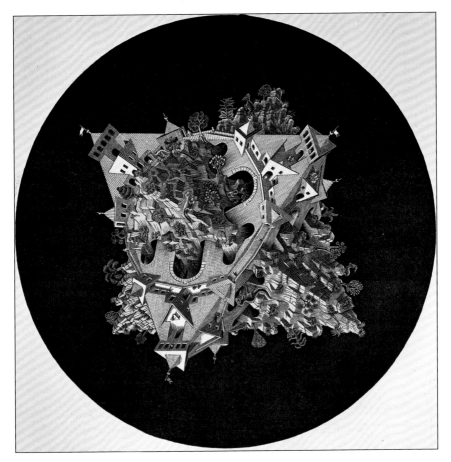

Plate 44

Plate 45

DROP (DEWDROP)
1948 Mezzotint
17.9 x 24.5 cm

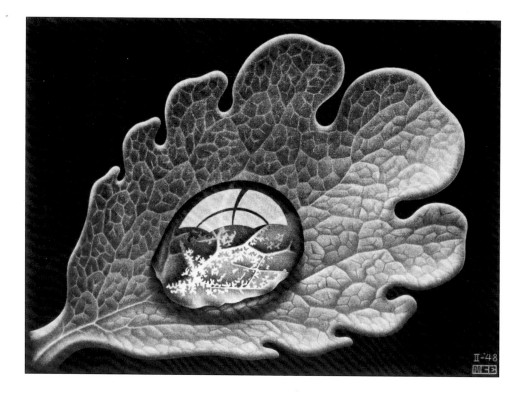

Plate 46

PLANE FILLING MOTIF WITH FISH AND BIRD

1951 linoleum cut
13.7 x 16.3cm

Plate 47

PREDESTINATION

1951 lithograph
29.4 x 42.2cm

Plate 48

TWO INTERSECTING PLANES

1952 woodcut in green, brown and black, printed from 3 blocks
22.4 x 31.0 cm

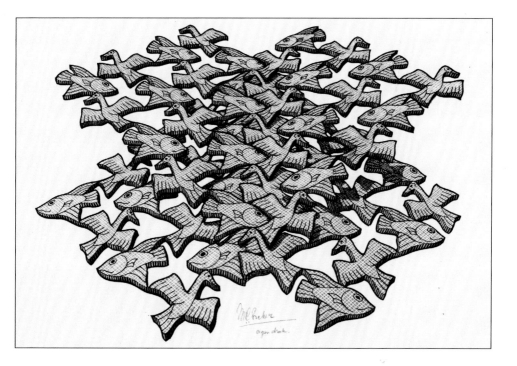

Plate 49

PUDDLE

1952 woodcut in black, green and brown, printed from 3 blocks
24.0 x 31.9cm

Plate 50

GRAVITY
1952 Lithograph and watercolor
29.7 x 29.7cm

Plate 51

CONCENTRIC RINDS
1953 wood engraving
24.1 x 24.1cm

Plate 52

RELATIVITY
1953 Lithograph
27.7 x 29.2cm

Plate 53

TETRAHEDRAL PLANETOIDE
1954 woodcut in green and black, printed from 2 blocks
43.0 x 43.0cm

Plate 54

LIBERATION
1955 lithograph
43.4 x 19.9cm

Plate 55

CONVEX AND CONCAVE
1955 Lithograph
27.5 x 33.5cm

Plate 56

RIND

1955 wood engraving and woodcut in black, brown, blue-grey and grey, printed from 4 blocks
34.5 x 23.5 cm

Plate 57

THREE WORLDS
1955 Lithograph
36.2 x 24.7 cm

Plate 58

WATER, NEW YEAR'S GREETING CARD
1956
15.5 x 13.5cm

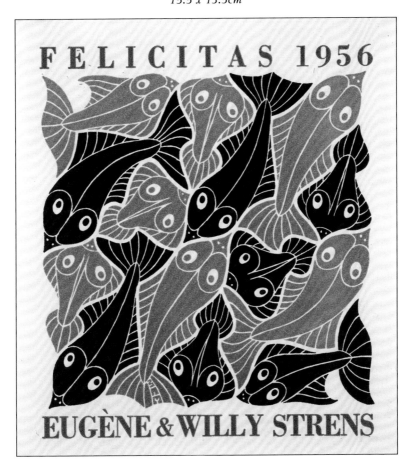

Plate 59

SMALLER AND SMALLER

1956 wood engraving and woodcut in black and brown, printed from 4 blocks
38.0 x 38.0cm

Plate 60

REGULAR DIVISION OF THE PLANE I

1957 woodcut in red
24.0 x 18.0 cm

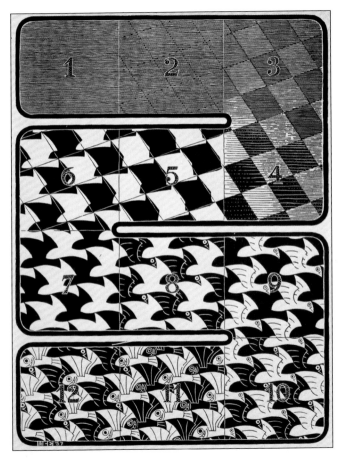

Plate 61

REGULAR DIVISION OF THE PLANE II

1957 woodcut in red
24.0 x 18.0 cm

Plate 62

REGULAR DIVISION OF THE PLANE III

1957 woodcut in red
24.0 x 18.0 cm

Plate 63

REGULAR DIVISION OF THE PLANE IV
1957 woodcut in red
24.0 x 18.0 cm

Plate 64

REGULAR DIVISION OF THE PLANE V

1957 woodcut in red
24.0 x 18.0 cm

Plate 65

BELVEDERE
1958 Lithograph
46.2 x 29.5cm

Plate 66

SPHERE SPIRALS

1958 woodcut in grey, black, yellow and pink, printed from 4 blocks
Diameter 32.0cm

Plate 67

ASCENDING AND DESCENDING

1960 Lithograph

35.5 x 28.5cm

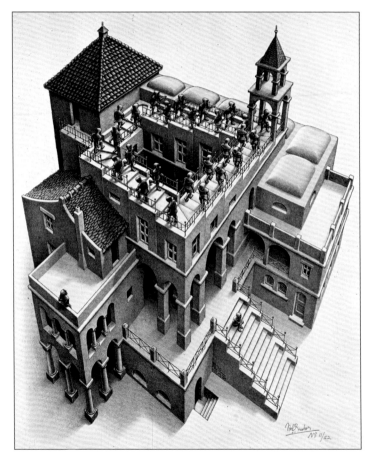

Plate 68

MOEBIUS STRIP I

1961 wood engraving and woodcut in red, green, gold and black, printed from 4 blocks
23.8 x 25.9cm

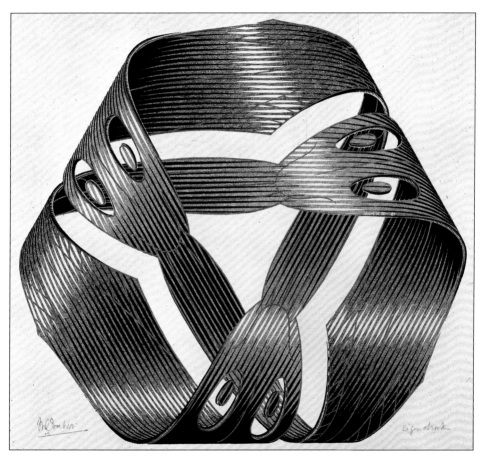

Plate 69

MOBIUS STRIP II (RED ANTS)

1963 woodcut
45.3 x 20.5cm

KNOTS

Plate 70

1965 woodcut in red, green and brown, printed from 3 blocks
43.0 x 32.0cm

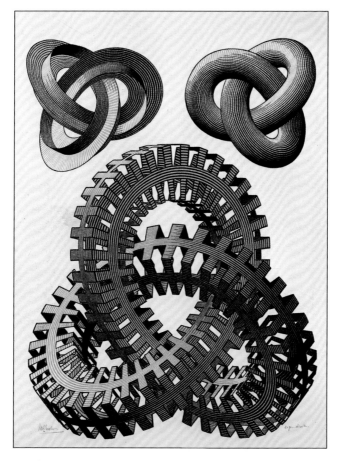

Plate 71

PATH OF LIFE III
1966 woodcut in red and black, printed from 2 blocks
36.6 x 37.1cm

Plate 72

SNAKES

1969 woodcut in orange, green and black, printed from 3 blocks
49.8 x 44.7cm

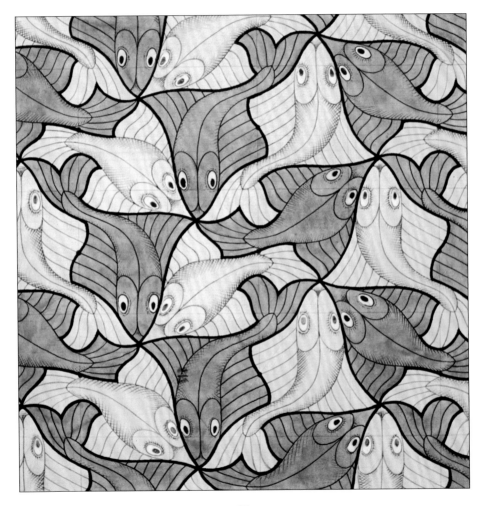

INDEX